thank you

for your purchase

Learn how to use this book
Use the QR code given or go to website below
https://www.2miletoolkit.com/guidehsrecordkeepingandplanning

Get in touch with us

 8108108550

 www.2MileToolkit.com

Order online
scan the QR code to view WhatsApp
catalogue and place an order

Our Homeschooling year ----------------------------------

MY POSITIVE AFFIRMATIONS

NAME OF MY CHILDREN & THEIR GRADE

FAVORITES

COLOR

FOOD

HOLIDAY

BOOKS & AUTHORS

Our Homeschool vision statement

SPIRITUAL

MIND & BODY

EDUCATIONAL

RELATIONSHIP

Year at a glance

(for best result start from the month you begin using this planner)

Month name

M	T	W	T	F	S	S

M	T	W	T	F	S	S

M	T	W	T	F	S	S

M	T	W	T	F	S	S

M	T	W	T	F	S	S

M	T	W	T	F	S	S

Year at a glance

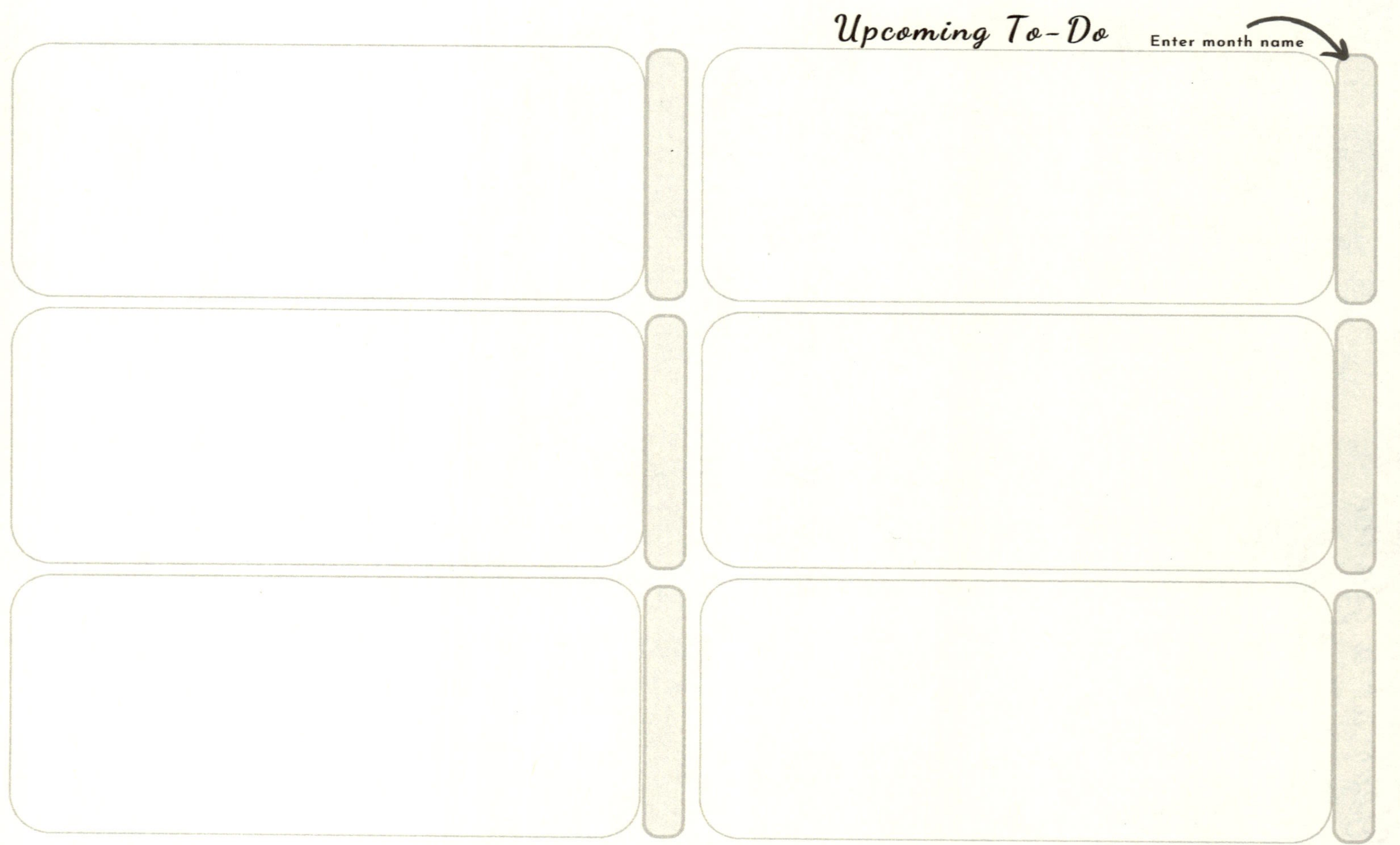

Upcoming To-Do
Enter month name

Upcoming To-Do

Notes
MON
TUE
WED

month of
SUN
SAT
FRI
THU

Attendance

CHILD NAME: _______

Days of the month

1					
2					
3					
4					
5					
6					
7					
8					
9					
10					
11					
12					
13					
14					
15					
16					
17					
18					
19					
20					
21					
22					
23					
24					
25					
26					
27					
28					
29					
30					
31					
TOTAL					

Attendance

CHILD NAME: _______

↪ Days of the month

Day	Col 1	Col 2	Col 3	Col 4	Col 5
1					
2					
3					
4					
5					
6					
7					
8					
9					
10					
11					
12					
13					
14					
15					
16					
17					
18					
19					
20					
21					
22					
23					
24					
25					
26					
27					
28					
29					
30					
31					
TOTAL					

Goals for the month

Learn inspired writings this month

Learn a song this month

Learn a character this month

Choose a character trait for the month. Write down the definition and an example to live it out.

Goals for the month

Notes
MON
TUE
WED

SUN

SAT

FRI

THU

Attendance

CHILD NAME: _______

Days of the month

	1	2	3	4	5	6
1						
2						
3						
4						
5						
6						
7						
8						
9						
10						
11						
12						
13						
14						
15						
16						
17						
18						
19						
20						
21						
22						
23						
24						
25						
26						
27						
28						
29						
30						
31						
TOTAL						

Attendance

CHILD NAME: __________

↱ Days of the month

	1	2	3	4	5
1					
2					
3					
4					
5					
6					
7					
8					
9					
10					
11					
12					
13					
14					
15					
16					
17					
18					
19					
20					
21					
22					
23					
24					
25					
26					
27					
28					
29					
30					
31					
TOTAL					

Goals for the month

GOALS	DONE

Learn inspired writings this month

Learn a song this month

Learn a character this month
*Choose a character trait for the month. Write down the definition and
an example to live it out.*

Goals for the month

GOALS	DONE

Notes
MON
TUE
WED

month of
SUN
SAT
FRI
THU

Attendance

CHILD NAME: ______________

Days of the month

1						
2						
3						
4						
5						
6						
7						
8						
9						
10						
11						
12						
13						
14						
15						
16						
17						
18						
19						
20						
21						
22						
23						
24						
25						
26						
27						
28						
29						
30						
31						
TOTAL						

Attendance

CHILD NAME:

↱ Days of the month

1						
2						
3						
4						
5						
6						
7						
8						
9						
10						
11						
12						
13						
14						
15						
16						
17						
18						
19						
20						
21						
22						
23						
24						
25						
26						
27						
28						
29						
30						
31						
TOTAL						

Goals for the month

GOALS	DONE

Learn inspired writings this month

Learn a song this month

Learn a character this month
Choose a character trait for the month. Write down the definition and an example to live it out.

Goals for the month

GOALS	DONE

Notes
MON
TUE
WED

month of
SUN
SAT
FRI
THU

Attendance

CHILD NAME: ___________

↻ Days of the month

1					
2					
3					
4					
5					
6					
7					
8					
9					
10					
11					
12					
13					
14					
15					
16					
17					
18					
19					
20					
21					
22					
23					
24					
25					
26					
27					
28					
29					
30					
31					
TOTAL					

EXTRA-CURRICULAR ACTIVITIES

CHILD NAME: _______________

Days of the month

1					
2					
3					
4					
5					
6					
7					
8					
9					
10					
11					
12					
13					
14					
15					
16					
17					
18					
19					
20					
21					
22					
23					
24					
25					
26					
27					
28					
29					
30					
31					
TOTAL					

Goals for the month

GOALS	DONE

Learn inspired writings this month

☐

Learn a song this month

☐

Learn a character this month

Choose a character trait for the month. Write down the definition and an example to live it out.

☐

☐
☐
☐
☐
☐
☐
☐
☐
☐
☐
☐
☐
☐
☐

Goals for the month

GOALS	DONE

Notes
MON
TUE
WED

month of
SUN
SAT
FRI
THU

EXTRA-CURRICULAR ACTIVITIES

Attendance

CHILD NAME: _______________

Days of the month

1						
2						
3						
4						
5						
6						
7						
8						
9						
10						
11						
12						
13						
14						
15						
16						
17						
18						
19						
20						
21						
22						
23						
24						
25						
26						
27						
28						
29						
30						
31						
TOTAL						

Attendance

CHILD NAME: __________

Days of the month →

1					
2					
3					
4					
5					
6					
7					
8					
9					
10					
11					
12					
13					
14					
15					
16					
17					
18					
19					
20					
21					
22					
23					
24					
25					
26					
27					
28					
29					
30					
31					
TOTAL					

Goals for the month

GOALS DONE

Learn inspired writings this month

Learn a song this month

Learn a character this month

Choose a character trait for the month. Write down the definition and an example to live it out.

Goals for the month

GOALS	DONE

Notes
MON
TUE
WED

month of
SUN
SAT
FRI
THU

Attendance

CHILD NAME:

↪ Days of the month

1						
2						
3						
4						
5						
6						
7						
8						
9						
10						
11						
12						
13						
14						
15						
16						
17						
18						
19						
20						
21						
22						
23						
24						
25						
26						
27						
28						
29						
30						
31						
TOTAL						

Attendance

CHILD NAME: ______

↻ Days of the month

	1					
2						
3						
4						
5						
6						
7						
8						
9						
10						
11						
12						
13						
14						
15						
16						
17						
18						
19						
20						
21						
22						
23						
24						
25						
26						
27						
28						
29						
30						
31						
TOTAL						

Goals for the month

GOALS	DONE

Learn inspired writings this month ☐

Learn a song this month ☐

Learn a character this month ☐
Choose a character trait for the month. Write down the definition and an example to live it out.

Goals for the month

Notes
MON
TUE
WED

month of
SUN
SAT
FRI
THU

1						
2						
3						
4						
5						
6						
7						
8						
9						
10						
11						
12						
13						
14						
15						
16						
17						
18						
19						
20						
21						
22						
23						
24						
25						
26						
27						
28						
29						
30						
31						
TOTAL						

Attendance

CHILD NAME: _______

→ Days of the month

EXTRA-CURRICULAR ACTIVITIES

Attendance

CHILD NAME: _______

→ Days of the month

	1	2	3	4	5	6
1						
2						
3						
4						
5						
6						
7						
8						
9						
10						
11						
12						
13						
14						
15						
16						
17						
18						
19						
20						
21						
22						
23						
24						
25						
26						
27						
28						
29						
30						
31						
TOTAL						

GOALS

DONE

Learn inspired writings this month ☐

Learn a song this month ☐

Learn a character this month ☐
Choose a character trait for the month. Write down the definition and an example to live it out.

GOALS

DONE

Notes
MON
TUE
WED

month of
SUN
SAT
FRI
THU

Attendance

CHILD NAME: _______

Days of the month

1					
2					
3					
4					
5					
6					
7					
8					
9					
10					
11					
12					
13					
14					
15					
16					
17					
18					
19					
20					
21					
22					
23					
24					
25					
26					
27					
28					
29					
30					
31					
TOTAL					

EXTRA-CURRICULAR ACTIVITIES

Attendance

CHILD NAME:

Days of the month

1						
2						
3						
4						
5						
6						
7						
8						
9						
10						
11						
12						
13						
14						
15						
16						
17						
18						
19						
20						
21						
22						
23						
24						
25						
26						
27						
28						
29						
30						
31						
TOTAL						

Goals for the month

GOALS	DONE

Learn inspired writings this month ☐

♪🎤 Learn a song this month ☐

Learn a character this month ☐
Choose a character trait for the month. Write down the definition and an example to live it out.

Goals for the month

GOALS	DONE

Notes
MON
TUE
WED

month of
SUN
SAT
FRI
THU

Attendance

CHILD NAME: _______

↻→ Days of the month

	1					
	2					
	3					
	4					
	5					
	6					
	7					
	8					
	9					
	10					
	11					
	12					
	13					
	14					
	15					
	16					
	17					
	18					
	19					
	20					
	21					
	22					
	23					
	24					
	25					
	26					
	27					
	28					
	29					
	30					
	31					
	TOTAL					

Attendance

CHILD NAME: __________

→ Days of the month

	1	2	3	4	5	6	7	8	9	10	11	12	13	14	15	16	17	18	19	20	21	22	23	24	25	26	27	28	29	30	31	TOTAL

Goals for the month

Learn inspired writings this month

☐

Learn a song this month

☐

Learn a character this month

Choose a character trait for the month. Write down the definition and an example to live it out.

☐

Goals for the month

GOALS	DONE
	☐

Notes
MON
TUE
WED

month of
SUN
SAT
FRI
THU

Attendance

CHILD NAME:

→ Days of the month

1						
2						
3						
4						
5						
6						
7						
8						
9						
10						
11						
12						
13						
14						
15						
16						
17						
18						
19						
20						
21						
22						
23						
24						
25						
26						
27						
28						
29						
30						
31						
TOTAL						

EXTRA-CURRICULAR ACTIVITIES

Attendance

CHILD NAME: _______

↪ Days of the month

1					
2					
3					
4					
5					
6					
7					
8					
9					
10					
11					
12					
13					
14					
15					
16					
17					
18					
19					
20					
21					
22					
23					
24					
25					
26					
27					
28					
29					
30					
31					
TOTAL					

Goals for the month

Learn inspired writings this month ☐

Learn a song this month ☐

Learn a character this month ☐
Choose a character trait for the month. Write down the definition and an example to live it out.

Goals for the month

GOALS	DONE

Notes
MON
TUE
WED

THU
FRI
SAT
SUN
month of

Attendance

CHILD NAME: ___________

(→ Days of the month

	1
	2
	3
	4
	5
	6
	7
	8
	9
	10
	11
	12
	13
	14
	15
	16
	17
	18
	19
	20
	21
	22
	23
	24
	25
	26
	27
	28
	29
	30
	31
	TOTAL

Attendance

CHILD NAME: _______

→ Days of the month

1					
2					
3					
4					
5					
6					
7					
8					
9					
10					
11					
12					
13					
14					
15					
16					
17					
18					
19					
20					
21					
22					
23					
24					
25					
26					
27					
28					
29					
30					
31					
TOTAL					

Goals for the month

<table>
<tr><td>GOALS</td><td>DONE</td></tr>
</table>

Learn inspired writings this month

Learn a song this month

Learn a character this month

Choose a character trait for the month. Write down the definition and an example to live it out.

Goals for the month

GOALS	DONE

Notes
MON
TUE
WED

month of
SUN
SAT
FRI
THU

EXTRA-CURRICULAR ACTIVITIES

Attendance

CHILD NAME:

Days of the month →

1						
2						
3						
4						
5						
6						
7						
8						
9						
10						
11						
12						
13						
14						
15						
16						
17						
18						
19						
20						
21						
22						
23						
24						
25						
26						
27						
28						
29						
30						
31						
TOTAL						

Attendance

CHILD NAME: _______

↪ Days of the month

	1	2	3	4	5	6
1						
2						
3						
4						
5						
6						
7						
8						
9						
10						
11						
12						
13						
14						
15						
16						
17						
18						
19						
20						
21						
22						
23						
24						
25						
26						
27						
28						
29						
30						
31						
TOTAL						

Goals for the month

Learn inspired writings this month

Learn a song this month

Learn a character this month

Choose a character trait for the month. Write down the definition and an example to live it out.

Goals for the month

GOALS	DONE

A glimpse into your year

Concepts learned

Top Accomplishments

A glimpse into your year

Challenge faced

What to change

About your child

Things I love about

About your child

Strength

Weakness

Needs

Reading/Viewing log

print book/movie/website/audio book/e-book details   DONE

Reading/Viewing log

print book/movie/website/audio book/e-book details

DONE

Subscription/Payment tracker

Service	Paid On	Period/ Due on	Amt

Subscription/Payment tracker

Service	Paid On	Period/ Due on	Amt

Field trip log

Date:	Location:

Date:	Location:

Date:	Location:

Field trip log

Date:	Location:

Date:	Location:

Date:	Location:

Budget

Keep a track of resources purchased for homeschooling purpose

MATERIALS	COST

Budget 

Keep a track of resources purchased for homeschooling purpose

MATERIALS	COST

Learning Materials

List all the materials you use to learn. This will help in budgeting for next year and also keeping a track of items that can now be donated.

SUPPLIES	BOOKS/CURRICULUM	LEARNING MATERIALS

Notes

Notes

Notes

Notes

Notes

Notes

Notes

Notes